Resurre
– fac
fic

ON Hugo used
nvisible friend called
kywalker to be precise.

Ever since meeting Luke in a film, Hugo chatted away to him and became very knowledgeable about this Jedi knight. Luke Skywalker kindly passed on his considerable knowledge of the Force to Hugo, so that together they would have marvellous adventures fighting for the Rebel Alliance. But (thankfully?) if pressed on the point of the existence of his invisible friend, Hugo would immediately back down and say it was just a game.

Luke was just a 'pretend friend' – a childhood fantasy – a projection of Hugo's imagination.

I also know a local man called Andrew who has an invisible friend. A few years ago, I thought it would be interesting to interview Andrew about his invisible friend in front of hundreds of people, including many Oxford academics. Andrew's invisible friend is called Jesus: Jesus Christ to be precise.

Andrew met Jesus in a book and claims to have great adventures with him. He talks to his invisible friend each day and claims to know him personally.

Just like Hugo, Andrew knows an awful lot about his invisible friend and, quite extraordinarily, claims that he is going to live with him when he dies.

Unlike Hugo, Andrew insists, when pressed on the matter, that his invisible friend is real. He will not back down and concede that it is made up, or is merely a projection to make life more meaningful.

You might say, "Well, good for him, if this Jesus thing enriches his life. We all have our personal quirks; talking to ourselves or living through an avatar in 'Second Life'. Andrew has merely taken it a step further."

I disagree entirely. It matters a great deal whether or not Andrew is right about his invisible friend Jesus! No doubt a well-developed imagination can be enormously beneficial, but it is surely a mark of insanity when a person can no longer distinguish fantasy from reality. We may all be inclined to build our castles in the air, but only the psychotic try to live in them.

Faith-heads or fantasists?

I know of no evidence to suggest that Andrew is mentally weak, let alone psychotic. Neither his job as professor of Material Physics at Oxford University nor his hobby of flying would mix well with a delusional frame of mind. Precision combined with a hard-headed application of accurate data is what is required of both a scientist and pilot. Unsurprisingly, Andrew is one of the sharpest thinking, fiercely logical people you could ever meet.

His approach (which is typical of scores of high-calibre Christian scientists) is at variance with Prof. Richard Dawkins' claim that faith is irrational:

"Dyed-in-the-wool faith-heads are immune to argument." Faith is a **"... process of non-thinking"**, which is **"... evil precisely because it requires no justification, and brooks no argument".**[1]

There are hundreds of millions of ordinary, sane people on this planet who believe that Jesus of Nazareth rose from the dead, is alive today and, though invisible, is a friend to whom they can talk, as real to them as a husband or wife.

You will probably know followers of Jesus – perhaps one of them gave you this little book. Wherever you live, study or work, you will find ordinary, rational, upright citizens, whether they be civil servants, students, factory workers, professors, accountants, musicians or sportsmen, all of them making the same astonishing claim: that Jesus is alive today. Rather than dismiss them as "faith-heads", why not do what the New Atheists suggest and refuse to allow Christianity to be "immune to argument" and left as "a process of non-thinking" which "requires no justification"? Why not engage with the claim they're making?

Outlandish lie or radical truth?

As the Apostle Paul said in one of the earliest and most well-attested manuscripts of the New Testament:

"If Jesus has not been raised from the dead, our preaching and your faith is futile ... and we apostles are liars ..."[2]

The ripples that continue to spread out across the world, transforming millions of ordinary and sane individuals into utterly dedicated followers of a man who died nearly two thousand years ago – surely they had to start somewhere?

What was the rock thrown into the water of human history from which all these ripples have come? What is it that gives these followers of Jesus such certainty that what they believe is objectively, factually true, rather than just "true for me"?

History offers us a single, clear answer. It all begins around an empty tomb in 1st-century Palestine and the confident proclamation by Jesus' first followers that Jesus Christ is alive having been killed and buried in a tomb.

Christianity is built on the stupendous assertion that Jesus, the man who claimed to be God, was crucified, dead and buried and on the third day rose bodily from the dead and appeared to his followers.

Death makes life absurd

In spite of its uncompromising inevitability, we find death deeply frightening, don't we? Life is like a relentless escalator on which we're running up the wrong way. Even though we know for sure that one day we will stumble and be thrown off, we do all we can to stay on as long as possible. The frightening thing is, we don't know when that moment will come. Two of my closest friends from university were dead before they reached 25. One died accidentally during a drug trip and another was killed in a car crash barely two years after graduation.

That escalator moves inexorably against you and one day, however invincible you might feel now, you will trip, and it will continue. With a pitiless indifference to your accomplishments, ambitions and the feelings of those who love you – it will throw you away.

The futility of death

"What should it profit you", asked Jesus, **"if you gain the whole world and lose your life?"**[3]

Our most thoughtful writers explore the absurdity of human ambition and aspiration in the light of our inevitable death.

Leo Tolstoy, in his short story, *How much land does a man need?*, introduces us to Pahom, a Russian peasant who finds himself listening to two sisters discussing the vexed question of how much do we need in life. "If I had plenty of land, I shouldn't fear the Devil himself!" says Pahom triumphantly.

In his quest for security, Pahom agrees a deal with simple landowners, namely that for the price of a thousand roubles (a paltry sum), Pahom can claim as much fertile land as he can walk around in a day. However, this claim is conditional on Pahom returning to the starting point before the sun sets. If he is too ambitious, and does not make it back before the sun goes down, he loses both his money and the land he has claimed.

Pahom sets off at a cracking pace and walks a great distance, trying to encircle as much land as possible. After covering a vast acreage, Pahom notices the sun beginning to set and, realising he could lose everything, embarks on a last, mad rush to return to the starting point. With a monumental effort he just makes it. Pahom has done it! Just as the sun sets in front of him he claims a huge tract of land, more than he had ever dreamed of owning. He will never be poor again.

Suddenly, he clutches at his chest. The physical exertion was too great for his heart, and he dies on the spot, surrounded by his newly acquired estate. His servant picks up the spade and digs a grave long enough to lay Pahom in.

The answer to Tolstoy's question "How much land does a man need?" is: "From his head to his heels" – that's how much land he needs.

"What should it profit us if we gain the whole world and lose our life?" Death is inevitable, relentless and brutal, and it mocks our very existence.

The Gospels – eyewitness, biographical reports of Jesus – reflect this stark reality in the accounts of Jesus' death. His followers became immediately dejected and dispirited. The whole Jesus thing was over. Even though it had been such an adventure, and in spite of Jesus' promises of eternal life, death had rendered even Jesus' life to be meaningless.

Additionally, the manner of Jesus' death had been so shameful and shocking that even his closest followers felt unable to go out in public. They hid behind a locked door, utterly downcast and ashamed.

Personal transformation

But, just a few days later, something changed Jesus' followers. Something transformed them from being craven cowards, hiding for their lives, into a fearless group of witnesses who could not be silenced, not even by brutality and torture and execution.

Within months of Jesus' death, the Roman colony of Palestine was in uproar and neither Jewish nor Roman authorities could put down the followers of Jesus. How do we account for such a dramatic transformation?

Jesus had not merely been killed, but totally humiliated and disgraced. 1st-century Jews regarded anyone who was crucified as scum and cursed by God. Whatever Jesus had achieved in his life was eclipsed by his disgusting death. It was so shameful that no follower of his could show their face in public. Even Peter, the most fiercely loyal disciple, denied any knowledge of Jesus and fled into hiding with the others.

Why then within a few weeks were these early Christians willing to die so painfully and shamefully themselves, rather than deny that Jesus had risen from the dead?

Something convinced them. Something transformed them. But what was it? Why was Peter willing to be brutally executed by Nero for his belief in Jesus, despite having been such a coward?

You might reply: "Oh, he died for the cause. Lots of people have died for religious causes."

On the surface it sounds like a reasonable explanation, but it is totally insufficient: the so-called cause had clearly ended for Peter on the night of Jesus' arrest. Peter had drawn his sword and was ready to fight to save him. Jesus rebuked him and told him to put away his sword. Peter was left hurt, deskilled and dejected. He had been willing to fight bravely for the cause – but the cause ended at the moment Jesus allowed himself to be arrested, tortured and murdered. Peter's denial of Jesus, just a few hours later, was surely inevitable. He didn't mind fighting for a cause, but there was no way he would die for a lost one.

What then managed to transform him, restore him and re-energise his courage and commitment? Why was Peter, who caved in at the taunts of a slave girl, willing to be crucified upside down rather than deny that Jesus was Lord?

Peter was changed by something solid, tangible and real.

He claimed it was his beloved Jesus who had been raised from the dead. Nothing less than that would turn a proud, broken man like Peter into a humble and fearless witness to the truth. Thousands of other Christians, similarly, were willing to be fed to wild animals, and sawn in half. They could not and would not deny that Jesus was alive, not even the ones who were nailed to crosses, then covered in tar and set on fire to light up Nero's botanical gardens.

Cultural Revolution

More remarkable still, many thousands of religious Jews came to follow Jesus after his death. To do so, they simply gave up Temple worship, animal sacrifice and Sabbath observance. They even accepted the Gentile followers of Jesus into their homes and meetings.

They were abandoning deep-set, permanent distinctives that had been integral to Jewish identity for centuries, and were more important to them than life and death. Nothing less than the bodily resurrection of Jesus could achieve such a radical, rapid and permanent cultural revolution.

Evidence for the resurrection

There are two main pieces of evidence for the resurrection of Jesus: the empty tomb and the subsequent appearances of the risen Jesus.

1 The empty tomb

The early church was sure the tomb was empty. Jesus' followers proclaimed it boldly in the hearing of unsympathetic religious leaders, who were well aware of what had just happened. Peter, in his first public sermon on the Jewish feast of Pentecost, appealed to the public knowledge of those who had actually killed Jesus.

"... you, with the help of wicked men, put him to death by nailing him

to the cross. But God raised him from the dead."[4]

Peter knew that these powerful men could turn on him for the slightest inaccuracy, yet he boldly appealed to their own local knowledge of events. You don't do that unless you are sure.

You don't risk public ridicule and torture if you are not convinced of the facts. It was clearly common knowledge that Jesus' tomb was empty.

The empty tomb has proved itself to be the stumbling block of every attempt to destroy Christianity down the ages. Its emptiness is uncompromising, since Jesus' tomb couldn't have been relatively empty.

A debate on the evidence for the resurrection took place at Edinburgh University several Easters ago. I debated with rationalist author Stewart Campbell, who made it clear to the five hundred students present that he believed the tomb of Jesus was empty, and acknowledged this as "common ground".

History tells us that the tribe called Christians first assembled around the empty tomb of Jesus of Nazareth. So we must consider the alternative explanations for the empty tomb and establish which, if any, has credibility.

Wrong tomb?

One theory suggests that the women followers of Jesus, who reported his body missing, had mistakenly gone to the wrong tomb – one that was empty and unused – and wrongly assumed that Jesus had been raised from the dead. The other disciples came to the same conclusion and began to preach, in full hearing of the authorities, that Jesus was raised from the dead, when in fact his body was in a nearby tomb. Thousands of others who were in Jerusalem at the time of Jesus' death also came to this mistaken conclusion and, on the basis of this mistake, became wholehearted followers of Jesus.

If this is how belief in the resurrection of Jesus started, we can be sure that the Jewish authorities, who (along with the Romans) were anxious to contain the followers of Jesus, would not have made the same mistake. They would not have forgotten in which of the prepared tombs they had placed the body of Jesus.

The authorities had placed Roman guards at Jesus' tomb – on pain of death – to prevent the body from being stolen. This being the case, the Jewish and Roman authorities (who became deeply troubled by reports of an empty tomb), would surely have little trouble in exposing this pathetic mistake.

All they needed to do was parade Jesus' body in public to scotch these rumours forever.

"It passes the bounds of credibility that the early Christians could have manufactured such a tale and then preached it among those who might easily have refuted it simply by producing the body of Jesus."[5]

Stolen body?

To counter the irrefutable evidence of the empty tomb, the religious authorities put out their own official lie, one they thought would be more credible and would explain why they couldn't produce the body of Jesus. They even paid the tomb guards to go along with it:

"... And when they had assembled with the elders and consulted together, they gave a large sum of money to the soldiers, and said, 'You are to say, "His disciples came by night and stole him away while we were asleep." And if this should come to the governor's ears, we will win him over and keep you out of trouble ...'"[6]

Whilst the guards slept (knowing they could be executed for this), Jesus' disciples quietly moved the half-tonne boulder to one side, unwrapped the body of Jesus and meticulously put the grave clothes back to look as if someone was still occupying them.

Please note that it is *sleeping* guards reporting all this!

The disciples then furtively hid Jesus body, came out of hiding and strode into Jerusalem proclaiming **"Jesus is alive, he is risen from the dead!"**

And so the persecution and torture begins, and thousands die for a dismal lie.

How could three thousand Jews who were in Jerusalem at this very time become Christians within five weeks of these events? They had access to all the main facts, not least that the tomb was empty! They certainly didn't believe the official Roman explanation.

Something big persuaded them to join the Christians, even though it meant losing so much of their heritage, wealth and – for many – their very lives. Does the grave robbery theory account for the joy, honesty and beautiful integrity of these first Christian martyrs?

People will sometimes die for a cause they believe to be true, but not for a miserable lie.

Notably, the conspiracy never broke. We know this since not one of Jesus' disciples was ever quoted as admitting to this. If they had, the religious authorities would have made much of it.

The swoon theory?

The one remaining theory to account for the empty tomb claims that Jesus never actually died. He just swooned from exhaustion, and loss of blood. The Roman centurion mistakenly released his body to be buried, and Jesus emerged from the tomb alive.

Having been horribly beaten to within an inch of his life, tortured, nailed to a cross for six hours, and having had a spear thrust into the side of his heart, Jesus is pronounced dead. The person who pronounced him dead would have been the Roman centurion, a leader of the most able killers in history – they knew what death looked like! Jesus' corpse is then bound up head to toe with many pounds of bandages soaked in ointments and spices, allowing the embalming fluid to be absorbed into his skin and open wounds.

Then (according to this theory), the cool air of the tomb revives Jesus. He removes the grave clothes (and folds them!), shifts the half-tonne boulder, eludes the watching guards and then tracks down the disciples who are cowering in a locked upper room.

As Jesus enters the room, they mistake this ghastly resuscitation for a glorious resurrection. And believe, on the basis of the disfigured remains in front of them, that Jesus is the glorious conqueror over death and Lord of all.

Does that explanation make any sense of what actually happened?

No established explanation

We should expect, if the resurrection of Jesus did not happen, that the actual truth – in the form of a single, convincing alternative explanation – would emerge from the enemies of the Christian church. Over time, this alternative explanation would become more and more established and would be used to counter the growth of this hated sect.

After all, history is written by the winners. But the earliest Christians were not winners: the message they preached was countercultural and they were perceived as a threat and were persecuted at every turn. Yet the claim these losers made was never decisively overturned. Instead, all that has emerged is a concoction of half-baked, fanciful theories that try to explain away the evidence rather than to engage with it.

All that these theories of a wrong tomb, grave robbery and a swooning Jesus have in common is the prior assumption that a resurrection could never happen, so surely any alternative is better, however implausible.

G.K. Chesterton's detective character, Father Brown, maintained that he found it easier to believe the impossible than he did the improbable:

"I'm exactly in the position of the man who said, 'I can believe the impossible, but not the improbable.'" "That's what you call a paradox, isn't it?" asked the other. "It's what I call common sense, properly understood," replied Brown. "It really is more natural to believe a supernatural story, that deals with things we don't understand, than a natural story that contradicts things we do understand. Tell me that the great Mr. Gladstone [the one-time Prime Minister], in his last hours, was haunted by the ghost of Parnell, and I will be agnostic about it. But tell me that Mr. Gladstone, when first presented to Queen Victoria, wore his hat in her drawing-room and slapped her on the back and offered her a cigar, and I am not agnostic at all. That is not impossible; it's only incredible ...."[7]

If you said to me that you had witnessed our own Queen, coming out of a side door from Stringfellow's night club, wearing a Lady Gaga black bustier and fish-net stockings, and that she snorted a line of cocaine before attacking two bouncers using kung fu kicks ... then I would refuse to believe you.

Your claim is not "impossible", for Her Majesty the Queen could easily access the clothes and drugs of her choosing, and could possibly become violent in a drug-induced state.

Nevertheless, from all we know of her character and reputation, we would find such a claim so implausible and improbable as to be utterly unbelievable.

Similarly, the suggestion that these frightened and honest disciples were transformed into fearless witnesses, whom none could silence, by a monstrous lie, and that from this deceit emerged the most significant force for good and for change that the world has ever experienced, must be rejected as being contrary to all evidence, common sense and our knowledge of human nature.

On the other hand, if these impressive and honest people maintain that Jesus has risen and are willing to die for it, then surely we should consider their evidence, however impossible it might sound to our western, post-Enlightenment sensibilities.

2 Resurrection appearances

The Apostle Paul, in the most copied manuscript of the New Testament church, refers to a period of 40 days after his crucifixion when Jesus appeared to individuals, groups and a crowd of five hundred.

During this period, John, in his eyewitness account (John's Gospel, chapter 20), records that Jesus first appeared to Mary Magdalene (a remarkable detail if John's account is fictitious, since a woman's testimony was then regarded as unreliable and not valid in law), then the disciples and finally Thomas.

Hallucinations?

Maybe they were just hallucinating. Maybe it was all wish fulfilment, as in *Peter Pan* when Tinkerbell dies. The disciples just screwed up their courage and said, "I believe, I believe, I believe." Sceptics have focused on the emotional state of Mary Magdalene when she mistook Jesus for the cemetery gardener,[8] and easily overlook that a sharp-minded tax collector, a hardened political zealot and down-to-earth fishermen were part of the crowd of followers who saw Jesus.

Two points are worth noting. First, how extraordinary, if John's account in any way elaborates the plain facts, that Mary – a woman and former prostitute – should be cited as a credible witness. Second, if Mary is hallucinating as part of some wish fulfilment, why does she not recognise the figure in front of her and instead wrongly assume it is the gardener?

We must conclude that five hundred witnesses, to whom the Apostle Paul appeals as living witnesses to the resurrection, were all hallucinating the same thing and subsequently were willing to be tortured and killed for this misty-eyed apparition.

To invoke the explanation of "hallucination" requires one to engage with what a hallucination is.

Several studies in hallucinations have demonstrated this to be utterly impossible.[9] A hallucination is an internal event, not a mirage, a trick of the light. One might claim that 500 people shared the same dream with more credibility than this. Even if all of these people were suffering from the same psychosis, their varying diets, personalities and age, not to mention the fact that they have their own individual brains, would mean that they simply could not all have hallucinated Jesus simultaneously.

The eyewitnesses to Jesus' resurrection were people of different temperaments, in different places, at different times, "hallucinating" a thoroughly unexpected encounter with the murdered Jesus. It's agreed that hallucinations conform to certain criteria, none of which is present here. Additionally, it is very unlikely that hallucinations could inspire the radical personal transformation of the disciples, even to the point of being willing to die for their faith. Nor do hallucinations explain the stubborn fact of the empty tomb.

Refusing to believe

"But it's just not scientific," you might be tempted to say, as if that settled the matter. "Dead people stay dead."

Consider this: If Jesus is who he claimed to be, the one his miracles, teaching and impact suggest he is, then surely – if he is God in human form – we should only be surprised that he died in the first place, not that he came alive again.

Bertrand Russell published a collection of papers entitled *Why I am not a Christian* (also the title of one of the papers). In it, he failed to address the resurrection of Jesus, which one person remarked would be like claiming to write an informed/comprehensive book about cricket and forgetting to mention batting.

A Cambridge undergraduate read *Why I am not a Christian* to justify his own

dismissal of Christianity. However, he was so profoundly disquieted at the lack of coherence in Russell's arguments against Christianity that he decided to read the Gospel accounts for himself.

As the historical Jesus walked off the pages of that New Testament, this young student became utterly convinced that Jesus of Nazareth could not be ignored. Now a barrister and Oxford academic, he has published a book on the evidence for the resurrection.[10]

I need to see for myself

You might say, "That's OK for all these disciples, but what about me? So much is at stake on this – why can't I see the physical, risen Jesus for myself?"

Unfortunately, you are about two thousand years too late. That is simply the nature of historical events. And while this feels like a forceful complaint, we need to recognise that it isn't a compelling argument. Besides which, unless you were a disciple, you wouldn't have recognised Jesus even if you had seen him in his risen form.

As you read the following few verses from John's eyewitness testimony of the resurrection, you will notice that the disciple Thomas had a similar complaint:

"Now Thomas (also known as Didymus), one of the Twelve, was not with the disciples when Jesus came. So the other disciples told him, 'We have seen the Lord!'

"But he said to them, 'Unless I see the nail marks in his hands and put my finger where the nails were, and put my hand into his side, I will not believe.'

"A week later his disciples were in the house again, and Thomas was with them. Though the doors were locked, Jesus came and stood among them and said, 'Peace be with you!' Then he said to Thomas, 'Put your finger here; see my hands.

Reach out your hand and put it into my side. Stop doubting and believe.'

"Thomas said to him, 'My Lord and my God!'

"Then Jesus told him, 'Because you have seen me, you have believed; blessed are those who have not seen and yet have believed.'

"Jesus performed many other signs in the presence of his disciples, which are not recorded in this book. But these are written that you may believe that Jesus is the Messiah, the Son of God, and that by believing you may have life in his name."[11]

Why does Jesus give Thomas a slight rebuke: "Stop doubting and believe"? And again "Because you have seen me, you have believed; blessed are those who have not seen and yet have believed."

Was it reasonable of Thomas to refuse to believe the eyewitness testimony of his closest friends? Surely the transformation of these scared and distraught people he knew so well should have been enough for him?

John explains that this eyewitness testimony is enough for all those subsequently reading his account. He explains that authentic faith comes from hearing the honest testimony of the Apostles and believing because of it:

"... these are written that you may believe that Jesus is the Messiah, the Son of God, and that by believing you may have life in his name."

Firm evidence, authentic belief

Thomas said to him, **"My Lord and my God!"**

Thomas is no longer doubting, but worshipping at the feet of his risen Lord.

Nothing less than the resurrection of Jesus can explain the remarkable transformation of Thomas and his friends. Nothing less can explain the transformation that was set to change the course of history forever.

What does it mean for us now?

1 **Jesus is who he claimed to be.**

If Jesus rose from the dead, his claim to be God in human form, to be "the way, the truth and the life" and so the only way to God, is established.

2 **His death achieved what Jesus said it would achieve.**

Jesus claimed that the only way in which a just and good God could forgive us and be in relationship with rebellious humans was by dying on a cross. It was only after the resurrection that Jesus' followers confidently preached that Jesus had defeated the great enemies of sin, death and hell. Sin can now be forgiven, hell is denied and death cannot hold followers of Jesus.

3 The human race has an eternal future and you and I can be part of it.

God the Son, Jesus, became a man just over two thousand years ago. After his resurrection, his body was physical and fully human but it was also imperishable. All followers of Jesus will be given resurrection bodies of the same sort: physical, recognisable and yet gloriously different. They will not wear out, grow tired or old.

God will make re-make this planet and, in Jesus, will dwell physically with us forever, helping us to rule and enjoy a new world in which there is no death, pain or tears.

The day death died

My sister's 11-year-old son David died from having tumours on his brain. The day before David died I read this passage to him as I sat by his bed in the hospice:

"Then I saw a new heaven and a new earth, for the first heaven and the first earth had passed away, and the sea was no more. And I saw the holy city, new Jerusalem, coming down out of heaven from God, prepared as a bride adorned for her husband. And I heard a loud voice from the throne saying, 'Behold, the dwelling place of God is with man. He will dwell with them, and they will be his people, and God himself will be with them as their God. He will wipe away every tear from their eyes, and death shall be no more, neither shall there be mourning, nor

crying, nor pain anymore, for the former things have passed away.'"[12]

Such was David's confidence in the resurrection of Jesus that he was able to step into the darkness of death without fear and with real joy. The cancer consultant who had treated David attended his funeral along with several colleagues. He remarked to my sister that he had never seen a child so unafraid of death, which is why he felt compelled to come to his funeral and find out what lay behind that.

Stop doubting and believe

If you would like to investigate further the key evidence for Christianity visit www.bethinking.org/booklets and choose from a variety of talks and articles.

There is no power in the universe so great as that of God's Spirit who raised Jesus from the dead and gives joy to a dying child like David. Are you willing to stop doubting and believe? If you are willing to make Jesus your Lord and your God you may find this prayer helpful.

Prayer

"Dear Lord Jesus, I believe that you died so that I could be forgiven. I am sorry that I have doubted and sorry that I have rejected you.

I believe that then you came back to life, so I know I can trust your promise of eternal life.

I want to live forever with you; thank you that now I can.

Amen

If you have prayed this prayer, speak to a Christian friend or go to our website www.bethinking.org/booklets and email us using "Contact us".

Footnotes

1 Richard Dawkins, *The God Delusion* (Bantam Press, 2006, pages 347-348).

2 1 Corinthians 15:14.

3 Mark 8:36.

4 Acts 2:23.

5 John Warwick Montgomery, *History and Christianity* (InterVarsity Press, 1972, page 78).

6 Matthew 28:12-14.

7 G.K. Chesterton, *The Penguin Complete Father Brown* (Harmondsworth: Penguin Books, 1981, page 402).

8 John 20:1-18.

9 Oliver Sacks, *Hallucinations* (Picador, 2012).

10 Charles Foster, *The Jesus Inquest* (LionHudson, 2006).

11 John 20:24-31.

12 Revelation 21:1-4.